# HOW
# BIG
## IS A
## WHALE?

Illustrated by
Michael Woods

Written by
Jinny Johnson

**Rand McNally**
**for Kids**

Books•Maps•Atlases

**A Marshall Edition**
Conceived, edited, and designed by
Marshall Editions, 170 Piccadilly, London W1V 9DD

Published in the United States of America by Rand McNally & Co., 1995

**Library of Congress Cataloging-in-Publication Data**
Johnson, Jinny.
    How big is a whale? / written by Jinny Johnson ; illustrated by
Michael Woods.
      p.  cm.
    "Rand McNally for kids."
    ISBN 0-528-83729-X
    1. Body size—Juvenile literature.  2. Animals—Juvenile
literature.  [1. Size.  2. Animals.]  I. Woods, Michael, 1943-
ill.  II. Title.
QL799.3.J64   1995
591.4—dc20                    94-47267
                                  CIP
                                  AC

**Managing Editor:** Kate Phelps
**Designer:** Ian Winton
**Art Director:** Branka Surla
**Editorial Director:** Cynthia O'Brien

Printed and bound in Italy
by Officine Grafiche De
Agostini – Novara

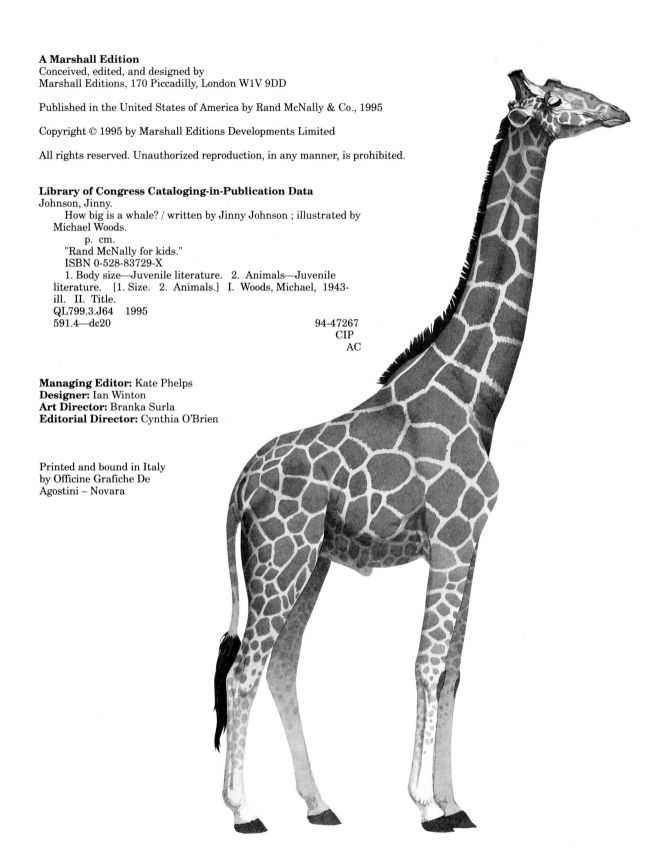

# Contents

# Which are the biggest insects?

The longest of all insects is a type of stick insect that lives in the hot jungles of Southeast Asia. Other big insects are the giant beetles that live in South American jungles. These include the hercules beetle, which is up to seven and a half inches long—about the same length as a banana.

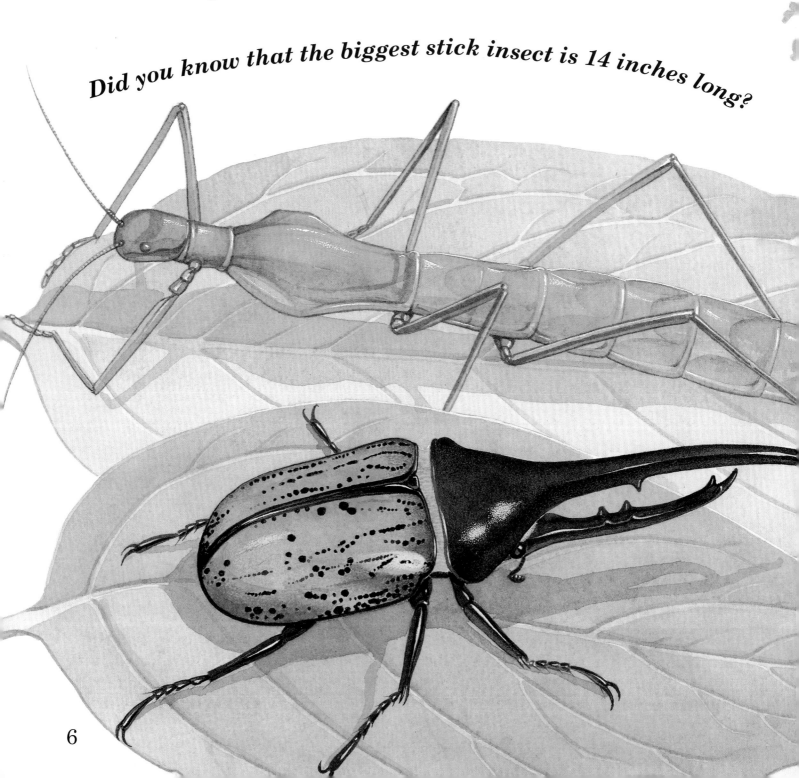

Did you know that the biggest stick insect is 14 inches long?

With its long slender body, the stick insect looks just like another twig as it sits in a tree. This helps keep it hidden from hunters such as birds.

The longest stick insect is nearly as long as a child's arm. Can you find the stick insect and child hidden here?

Male hercules beetles have long horns that are the same length as their bodies. They use these horns in battles with other males.

# How big is the biggest butterfly?

Some of the largest of all butterflies are the birdwings which live in jungles. Biggest of all is the female Queen Alexandra's birdwing, which measures up to 11 inches across with its wings fully spread. The male is smaller than the female and more brightly colored.

Tiny butterflies such as the Sonoran blue (above) and the Cassius blue (below) measure less than three-quarters of an inch across. But some moths are so small that several could fit on your fingernail.

The Queen Alexandra's birdwing is much bigger than an average-sized butterfly such as a red admiral. Can you find the eight red admirals hidden in the birdwing?

Birdwing butterflies live high in jungle trees where they eat nectar—a sugary liquid made by flowers. These beautiful butterflies are now very rare and it is against the law to take them from the wild.

*Did you know that a Queen Alexandra's birdwing butterfly is this big?*

A red admiral butterfly is about two inches across.

# Which is the biggest spider?

The giant of the spider world is the female goliath bird-eating spider. Her hairy body measures up to 4 inches and her legs spread across 11 inches. The male is a little smaller. These spiders live in the jungles of South America. They stay hidden under leaves and stones during the day and come out at night to hunt.

A bird-eating spider is bigger than a bird such as a wren. A wren is about four inches long.

Although this spider is called a bird-eating spider, it probably catches more snakes, lizards, and frogs than birds.

*Did you know that a goliath bird-eating spider is this big?*

The goliath bird-eating spider weighs three or four ounces. It is almost as heavy as an apple.

A common house spider in Europe and North America is usually less than an inch long. It is tiny compared to the bird-eating spider.

# Which is the biggest bird?

The ostrich is the biggest of all birds. It stands nine feet high, much taller than an adult human, and weighs as much as 350 pounds. Even its eye is bigger than the world's smallest bird—the bee hummingbird.

A male bee hummingbird is only a little more than two inches long. Can you see one hidden in the eye of the ostrich?

Although the ostrich has wings it cannot fly. Its body is too big and heavy to lift into the air. But it is a fast runner. It can race along at more than 45 miles an hour—faster than any other bird can run.

A female ostrich lays the biggest eggs of any living creature. An ostrich egg can weigh nearly four pounds.

An ostrich egg is six to seven inches long. A hen's egg is much smaller—it is only about two and a half inches long.

*Did you know that an ostrich's egg is this big?*

The egg of the bee hummingbird is the smallest laid by any bird. This tiny egg is just over a quarter of an inch long.

13

# Which bird has the biggest wings?

The wandering albatross has longer wings than any other bird. When fully spread, its wings measure nearly 12 feet from tip to tip. Its long wings help the albatross soar for miles over the southern oceans as it searches for food.

Can you find the three five-year-olds hidden on the wings of the albatross? They show just how huge this bird is.

Did you know that the wandering albatross can fly 300 miles a day on its huge wings?

14

Fish and squid are the main foods of the wandering albatross. The bird swoops down to the sea to seize its prey. It also follows ships and picks up food that is thrown overboard as garbage.

The wandering albatross spends most of its life in the air. It comes to land only to lay its eggs and care for its young.

A common pigeon, or rock dove, looks small next to the huge albatross. Its wings measure about two feet from tip to tip.

# Which bird has the biggest nest?

The largest tree nests are made by bald eagles. The biggest ever seen was more than 9 feet wide and nearly 20 feet deep. The bald eagle builds its nest with sticks and branches and lines it with soft grass.

Bald eagles catch fish to eat as well as birds and small animals. First the eagle watches until it spots a fish in the water. Then it swoops low and seizes the fish in its strong claws.

Both the male and female bald eagles are kept busy bringing food to their hungry young in the nest.

Did you know that a giraffe could fit into the biggest bald eagle's nest?

Bald eagles do not live in their nest all year round. They use it as a safe place in which to lay their eggs and keep their young. Nests are often used year after year. Each time more twigs and sticks are added.

The tiniest nest of all is made by the bee hummingbird. Its nest is only about an inch wide— about the size it is shown here.

17

# How big is the biggest fish?

The largest fish in the world is the whale shark. The biggest one ever measured was more than 41 feet long and probably weighed as much as 15 tons—more than three elephants.

Great white sharks are much smaller than whale sharks, but they are the largest of the fierce, hunting sharks.

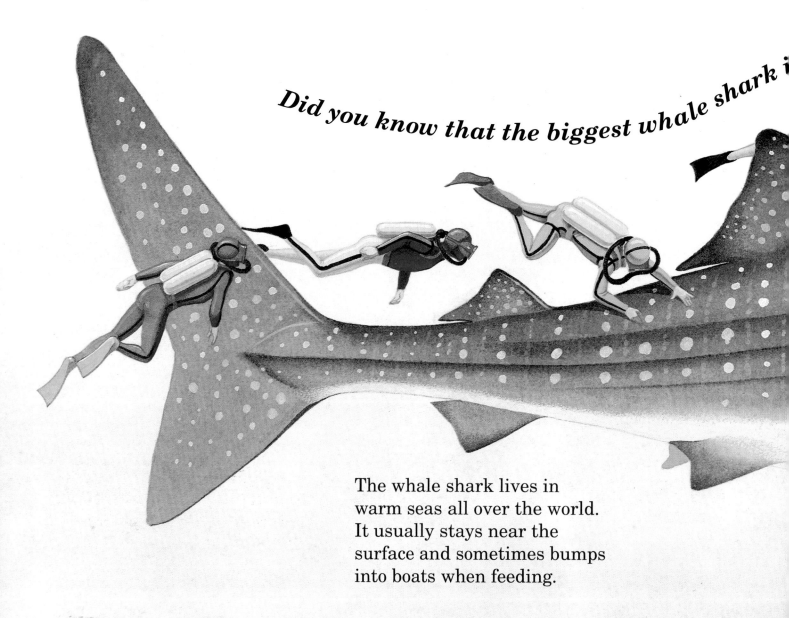

*Did you know that the biggest whale shark i*

The whale shark lives in warm seas all over the world. It usually stays near the surface and sometimes bumps into boats when feeding.

The whale shark is not a dangerous hunter like most other sharks. When feeding, the whale shark opens its mouth wide to take in lots of tiny fish and shrimp as well as sea water. When the shark closes its mouth again, the water drains out through the slits at the sides of its head, leaving the food behind.

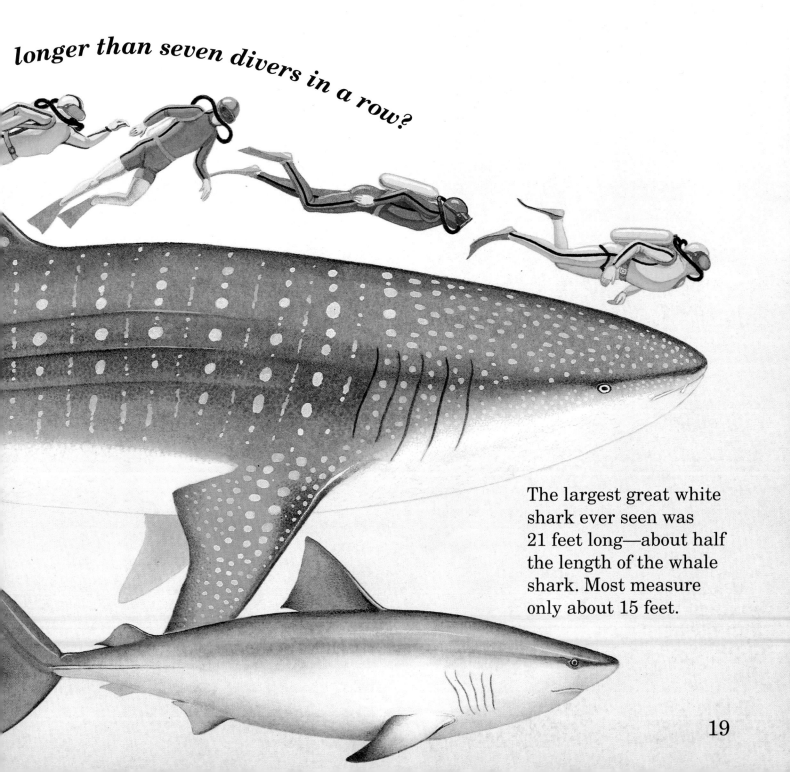

longer than seven divers in a row?

The largest great white shark ever seen was 21 feet long—about half the length of the whale shark. Most measure only about 15 feet.

# Which is the longest snake?

The longest of all snakes is the reticulated python. Most are more than 20 feet long but the biggest reticulated python ever seen measured more than 32 feet—nearly as long as three cars. The python is not a poisonous snake. It kills the animals it catches by wrapping them in its strong body until they are crushed to death.

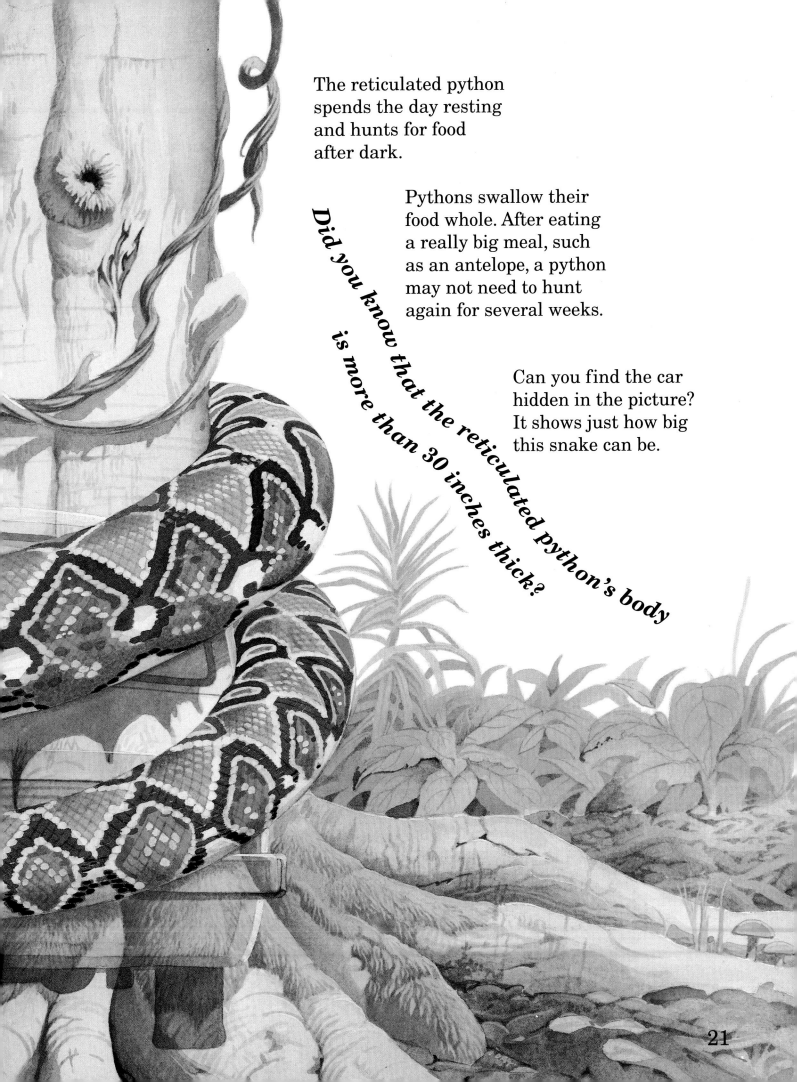

The reticulated python spends the day resting and hunts for food after dark.

Pythons swallow their food whole. After eating a really big meal, such as an antelope, a python may not need to hunt again for several weeks.

Can you find the car hidden in the picture? It shows just how big this snake can be.

Did you know that the reticulated python's body is more than 30 inches thick?

21

# How big is the biggest big cat?

The tiger is the biggest of all cats. It measures more than 10 feet from its nose to the tip of its tail. Not all tigers live in hot jungles. The biggest live in cold, snowy Siberia, which is part of Russia.

Tiger cubs usually stay with their mother for several years. During this time, the cubs learn how to hunt and take care of themselves.

Just like a pet cat stalking a bird, a hunting tiger creeps up on animals such as deer and wild pigs. When the tiger has gotten as close as possible, it pounces on its prey.

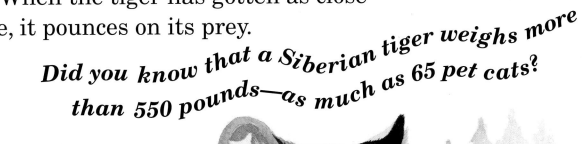

*Did you know that a Siberian tiger weighs more than 550 pounds—as much as 65 pet cats?*

A tiger's stripes help keep it hidden in grass and leaves when it is hunting.

# How tall is a giraffe?

The giraffe is the tallest of all land animals. A male giraffe can measure up to 19 or 20 feet from its feet to the horns on the top of its head.

Because giraffes are so tall, they can eat leaves at the tops of trees that other animals cannot reach. The giraffe strips leaves, buds, and fruit off trees with its lips and long tongue. A giraffe's tongue measures up to 17 inches—almost as long as the arm of an adult person.

Giraffes have good eyesight. This helps them watch out for enemies such as lions. They defend themselves by kicking out with their big hooves.

The biggest giraffes are as tall as four young people standing on each other's shoulders. Can you see the children hidden in this tree?

No two giraffes have exactly the same markings. Each one is slightly different.

# How big is an elephant?

The African elephant is the biggest land animal alive today. An elephant's tusk alone is as heavy as an adult person. A male elephant weighs nearly five tons. Females are smaller—about half the weight of males.

An elephant eats leaves, twigs, fruit, roots, and grass. It needs more than 400 pounds of food a day— that's about the same as 1,200 apples.

Even though they are very big, elephants are gentle animals. Mothers and young stay together in herds.

*Did you know that an elephant weighs as much as 35 pigs?*

An elephant has a trunk instead of a nose. The trunk is used for many things, including smelling, drinking, gathering food, and stroking young.

# How big is a whale?

The blue whale is the biggest animal that has ever lived. A full-grown blue whale is about 100 feet long, and its tongue alone is heavier than an elephant. Although blue whales are so huge, they eat only tiny shrimp called krill. One blue whale eats about four million of these shrimp every day.

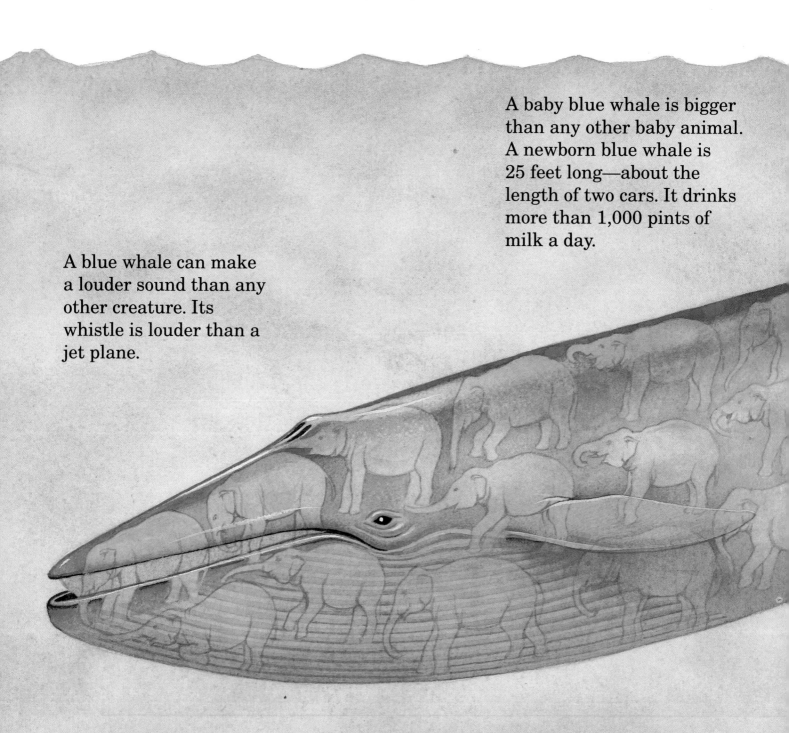

A baby blue whale is bigger than any other baby animal. A newborn blue whale is 25 feet long—about the length of two cars. It drinks more than 1,000 pints of milk a day.

A blue whale can make a louder sound than any other creature. Its whistle is louder than a jet plane.

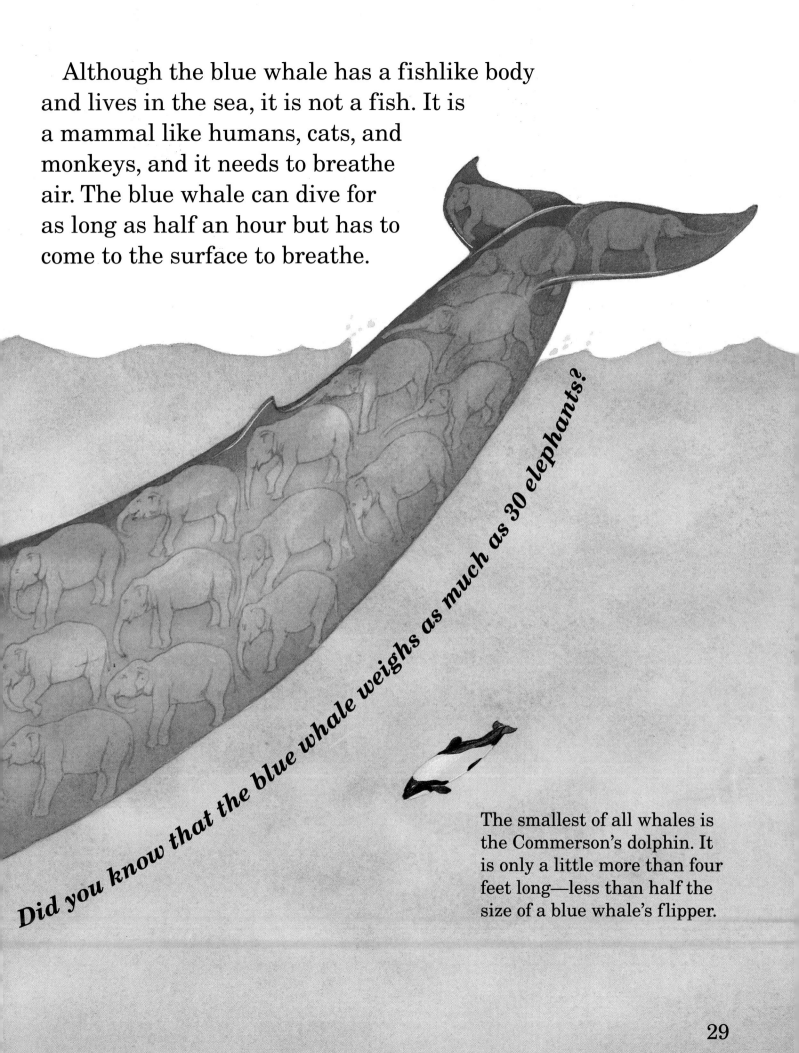

Although the blue whale has a fishlike body and lives in the sea, it is not a fish. It is a mammal like humans, cats, and monkeys, and it needs to breathe air. The blue whale can dive for as long as half an hour but has to come to the surface to breathe.

Did you know that the blue whale weighs as much as 30 elephants?

The smallest of all whales is the Commerson's dolphin. It is only a little more than four feet long—less than half the size of a blue whale's flipper.

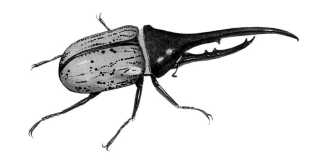

# Index